Contents

Foreword from the Bishop of Chichester

The churchyards of Sussex are places where we invest some of our most precious possessions.

Most obviously, these are the places where we invest memory and the narrative of a local community's history, because they hold the mortal remains of those we love. In that respect they are not simply the graveyards of the dead: they tell us what we today have inherited.

In many cases, these consecrated spaces also invite rest of a different kind. Each year, thousands of walkers visit our churches and find rest on their journey.

The environment of church and churchyard speaks of repose and refreshment. They invite investment in Christian faith. In mood and atmosphere they speak of what is core to Christian belief: the words of Jesus, "Come to me all ye that are heavy laden and I will give you rest."

The Nature of God's Acre project is doing an outstanding job of ensuring that we understand and value these varied aspects of our churchyards.

As safe places in which to invest, they also offer to nature an environment in which its flourishing can remind us of the Christian conviction that the resurrection points to the recovery of Eden and paradise, even now in this life.

So step into another world. Learn, in God's acre, to rest in peace and rise in glory.

+Martin Cicestr:

The Nature of God's Acre

Churchyards are beautiful places. They are also unique; they are neither gardens, fields nor parks. They are owned by the Church but belong to the community. Above all they are the places where generations past have found their rest. But it is not just the generations of people who have found their rest in these places – plants and animals increasingly pushed out from other surroundings, through development and changes in agricultural practice, have also found a haven.

Through the work of organisations such as Caring for God's Acre (details about whom are included at the end of this book), this role for churchyards has increasingly been recognised both by those interested in nature conservation, those charged with the maintenance of these places and by visitors, friends and relatives of those buried there.

Recently a small team came together interested in understanding how this latter group of people, those with a personal interest in churchyards, related to the nature there. The intention was to try to understand not just the particular plants and animals they liked or found intrusive, but also how nature impacted on their experience of the churchyard.

The team created the project The Nature of God's Acre to look empirically at these people's experience and to record their preferences and words, in order to better understand our relationship with nature in our churchyards today. The project team have been largely based in Sussex and with the support of the Bishop of Chichester, and some committed members of the churches we approached, we have been able to obtain responses from across Sussex.

This information has been supplemented by photographs of the churchyards involved, follow up interviews with volunteer questionnaire responders and additional information we found on the ecology of, and stories about, the churches and churchyards. The questionnaires and interviews have been analysed and reflected upon to give both a statistical response about people's experience of nature in churchyards and also a theological one.

We hope the outcomes from this work will be of value to those who work with and enjoy churchyards across Sussex – by comparing others' thoughts and views – and may possibly lead to one or two new destinations being added to their itinerary the next time they are visiting churchyards. In addition we hope the work will be of a wider value to the Church and other organisations involved in managing churchyards, to those with an interest in people's engagement with ecology (such as conservation organisations) and to those engaged in theological reflection on the subject.

From whichever perspective you come to view this book, we hope you enjoy and feel enlightened by its contents.

The Nature of God's Acre Team

The Revd Dr Mark Betson
Mark has a PhD in Hydrogeology and worked as an Environmental Scientist with ADAS before training for the ministry. He grew up largely in the small East Sussex village of Three Oaks and still has family there. Mark works currently as the Rural and Environment Officer for the Diocese of Chichester and is priest-in-charge of the parish of Lower Beeding with two churches and open churchyards.

Keith Datchler OBE
Keith is an agricultural estates manager in Sussex with a passion for conservation, particularly ancient meadows. He is a Founder Trustee of the High Weald Landscape Trust, previously Trustee of the Grassland Trust, Member of the Coronation Meadows Steering Committee and a Member of the Weald Meadows Partnership.
He was awarded an OBE in 2009 for services to conservation.

Miles King BSc. MSc FLS MCIEEM
Miles has worked in nature conservation for 28 years, holding senior positions in a number of conservation charities. He writes about nature conservation policy, politics and ethics and is interested in the relationship between nature and people, the places people share with nature and how the connection can be re-established, where it has been broken.

Michael Rudman DL
Michael has lived in the East Sussex countryside for over 40 years. Having been a London businessman, he is now a farmer and has always had a keen interest in biodiversity. As Chairman of the Spencer-Wills Trust, he has sponsored a number of countryside projects.

Sara Stonor DL
Sara has a life time involvement with the Church of England. She is a Lay Member of Chapter at Chichester Cathedral with responsibility for Cathedrals' Links to Parishes. She is on the Chichester Diocesan Synod and is a former Churchwarden of a rural parish. She is passionate about rural life and the biodiversity of churchyards.

Summary and Recommendations

First and foremost with this project we need to thank all those who volunteered the information to make it possible, because they are at the heart of this work – the book is about their personal response to the nature in churchyards.

Their input suggests the majority of people value the wildlife in their churchyard when they visit. This is by no means universal and the extent to how much people value the wildlife varies, but the message is clear that its presence is an asset to churchyards for most people. These people are not just those who go to the churches on a Sunday morning but many from the local community and beyond – walkers and tourists. This asset is one not just for the church, but for the whole community.

From the responses we received, many people strongly agreed that they felt peaceful, happy and relaxed when they saw wildlife in their churchyard. A large number also indicated having a spiritual feeling, being thoughtful and contemplative when they saw such wildlife. These responses suggest there is a link between the experience of nature in churchyards and wellbeing; one way of explaining why people value nature there. A deeper reflection was also present in the connection people made with nature – the cycle of life provided particular comfort for those contemplating issues of mortality.

However, from history (see later), it is recognised that the wildlife present in churchyards is not a product of them being left 'wild', but rather from their careful management. Their maintenance has in a large part determined the wildlife they now contain. This then leads on to the first recommendation from this work: **where possible churchyards should be managed to enhance their wildlife potential to support the wellbeing of those who visit**.

We recognise this is a challenging task for reasons of manpower and coming up with a sensitive management plan. In responding to this we hope that the role of a churchyard as a community asset will be recognised and supported through community volunteers and organisations, such as the Parish, District and County Councils. Opportunities should be sought to link churchyards with areas of high nature value such as, in Sussex, the South Downs National Park and Ashdown Forest.

Caring for God's Acre has a long track record of producing sensitive management plans for churchyards and, through a Heritage Lottery grant in 2012, has been able to roll out their experience nationally through a number of regional training events. We encourage churches and other interested organisations to engage with them in developing a management plan for their churchyards.

Our second recommendation as part of this work is: **to research further the role nature plays in the wellbeing of those who visit churchyards**.

Our research has been limited by funding, time and geography but has demonstrated that people's experience in churchyards is generally affected by the presence of wildlife, and that their experience of it is a positive one. However, can we go beyond that and look more closely at the type of experience? How does that experience compare with experiences elsewhere, both outside Sussex and also with other significant sites of natural beauty?

These are all questions which help understand the human condition and in particular our links to the nature and heritage contained in our churchyards. Comprehending our place in the cycle of life is a huge challenge on a personal level and churchyards could play a significant role in meeting that.

A Personal View by Keith Datchler

I grew up in London in a very confined and angular place. Everything seemed to be bounded and ridged. Before leaving the house, trousers were belted on, shirts buttoned-up, even my feet had to be tied into shoes. The garden had a hard edge where the grass met the path, as did the flowerbed where it joined the grass. Ninety degree edges to steps lead to hard pavements – straight lines and hard edges were everywhere. Even the green oasis of park had its edged path; where trees met grass was clean and defined. A "Keep Off The Grass" regime restricted freedom in all directions.

My Grandmother lived with us: she was 18 stones of pure affection, but, as all good things, it came to an end when she decided to move to the country. I thought my world might end but in reality it would be opened in a way no eight year old could ever predict.

From that point on, my six-week summer break was spent with her in the country. I remember more than anything the softness of the landscape; there were no hard edges. Everything blended; even the roadside verge softened the tarmac, hedges graduated into field, fields rolled over the landscape, woodlands were not square they almost trickled into valleys or clung to hillsides. I felt correct here in a way I had never experienced before; it fitted my body.

I had no corners or edges; I was rounded in the same way. I fitted this environment.

I can remember as if it were yesterday taking off my shoes to stand in a pond trying to catch the inhabitants. Suddenly I had a flush of senses I had never had – my feet were interpreting the world, feeding me information: Soft mud…insect wriggling…cold… how much support might the bottom layers offer?

As I moved to dry land, toes could grip – my feet were processing information about the ground constantly. Nobody taught me this, but I understood it all instantly, perfectly.

Nobody ever has to tell us to duck or crouch down if a sudden noise or danger challenges, we just do it instinctively. I discovered so much that first summer about myself as an animal species.

The joy of a skylark song; no danger; you look up, open yourself; the instinctive turn of my head if a blackbird or pheasant called the alarm.

One beautiful, early summer day I wondered into a meadow. A sea of colour alive with insects – the hairs on my arms went up. I made myself small, instinctively; not from fear of danger but out of respect and awe. I took off my shoes and socks again and reached out with my fingers, I needed all my senses to be immersed in this environment.

My life moved on and my parents eventually moved to the country. I would become a farmer, the product of an agricultural college in the sixties.

That time was all about food production – Produce, Produce, Produce; push the earth to yield up its bounty as if it were inexhaustible.

The estate I eventually came to manage had a small, unproductive farm on it; it had been farmed for decades by generations of the same family. They retired and I had to incorporate this land into the wider estate.

It was February – I stood looking at this neglected array of tiny fields, at a loss. How could we bring these into production and at little cost? I suddenly knew what to do: shut them up for a hay crop!

I returned the following June to see how things were looking. Nothing could have prepared me for what I saw; here was my childhood again – a flower-filled tapestry.

I experienced that indefinable reaction, this time as an adult. I asked myself what is happening. Am I simply remembering a childhood moment or is this a deeper memory?

That night I watched our dog turn a circle on the carpet before lying down, crushing the imaginary grass or reeds to make a bed. Here is a creature evolved and domesticated, the wolf long gone – bred and re-bred. Yet still it turns a circle: this is not a memory, as we know it. Instinct? Perhaps, or a genetic memory.

Had I experienced a genetic memory back then as a child in that meadow, without education or predefined prejudices? Had I just experienced it again as an adult when suddenly exposed to this pristine grassland that our ancient ancestors came down out of the trees to exploit? Indeed, we stood up and became bipedal to walk out across grassland.

Do we have our own "turning dog" in our genetic memory? If so, surely we should listen to that turning dog.

What has any of this to do with churchyards?

Our survey found that the flowers of the meadow caught our responders' attention the most. Is this subconscious recognition of a favoured habitat? Could this be our turning dog?

How obvious really that we can relate so intimately with nature when we are contemplative, or seeking emotional reassurance. I also found it so interesting that no one wanted the older part of the churchyard straightened or cleaned up. Yes, some preferred tidiness, but that natural relaxation of stone as it tips to one side over time or the encroachment of moss and lichen that softens even rock; these things were left unsaid, accepted.

As a layman I see these as places for letting go of loved ones, coming to terms with grief while cherishing the memory. Of marking out a life, yet seeing them carried forward to the next generation. Where the earth puts its arms around us and holds us for eternity till we become part of the earth itself. It is right that nature should watch over this precious acre.

To see so clearly that that isn't there
No touch can reach across the void
Words no longer spoken but the voice will always be heard
Listen, listen, tell the future of the past
Take all those that have been, to those yet to come
This is love eternal.

The View from the Churchwarden

On receiving the initial request to conduct a survey, my heart fell – yet another task to do! However, I was sensible of the support given to your project and after receiving permission from our Rector John Gay, moved it onto the 'To Do' list. Whilst considering how to approach the matter, I received a 'peace' about the project and was able to see it as an opportunity for 'outreach'.

I decided rather than make telephone calls to find people who had pictures; I might as well take the pictures myself. On doing this at the end of a day, I was met by the sight of something white moving in front of me. I tried to be as quiet as possible but, alas, the animal was aware of me and I was unable to get a photograph. I became aware of the quietness around me, apart from birdsong; a special place to be! It looked like a squirrel but to my (limited) knowledge this couldn't be correct. However, further investigation revealed that there are white squirrel(s) in Slinfold, but rarely seen; I felt privileged and the experience was gained because of your survey.

By kind permission taken from a letter by Mrs G Collier-Morgan, Churchwarden of St Peter's, Slinfold, about the Nature of God's Acre project.

Introduction to the Project

Churchyards are often ancient places. Their known history can be traced back to Saxon times, to the earliest wooden churches. Archaeology takes us further back to show these places were already being used in Roman and more ancient, pre-historic times. They occupy places of significance in the landscape – where a number of ancient trackways meet, where a track crosses a river or on a local high point with commanding views. They may have been the kernel around which villages developed, after the Romans left in 410AD and the arrival of Christianity shortly afterward. Their ancient links make them important to local communities, central to those communities' sense of identity. Their sacred links to the church strengthen that sense of great value.

These ancient places were very small. They started out as 'littens' (see entry for St Mary, East Preston) – the Saxon word for cemetery, but perhaps more accurately called God's Acre. A litten was the area of a customary acre, that is the area one man could plough in a day, in the furlongs of the Saxon open field farming system. This is about two thirds of a modern acre, if there is such a thing. The litten would have been partly protected from livestock, by earth banks often hedged around. Burials were marked with wooden crosses, which naturally disappeared, and plots were used and re-used. There was no sense of individual burials in these highly communal Saxon villages. As the littens were created from the surrounding land, they enclosed the nature of that land – the flowers, insects, birds and toadstools. Naturally the Saxons would not have wanted trees or shrubs to encroach, so a combination of mowing by scythe and grazing by local livestock would have kept the littens open. These activities inevitably created what we now know as wildflower meadows.

It is not too fanciful to think that Saxon littens are some of our oldest wildflower meadows. In the open field countryside of Saxon times, meadows were very unusual. Those that did exist were generally on wet ground by rivers and streams, where it was too wet to plough, and where the constant winter flooding created the flat ground and provided the fertility (via silt deposits) that made mowing for hay by scythe both possible and productive. That hay would then have been fed to cattle to keep them alive over the winter, when grazing was hard.

As the centuries past, the countryside changed again and again. Wildflower meadows had their heyday in the era of the ox and then horse, when they provided the fuel which ran the country, before steam and the internal combustion engine. In the 20th century, modern farming techniques and the drive to increase food production saw wildflower meadows disappear almost completely from the British countryside. Now the Weald is one of the last strongholds for wildflower meadows. Throughout this time and these tumultuous changes, the meadows of the littens, or churchyards as we now know them, have survived, more or less unscathed.

Few (though there is at least one in Sussex) are grazed by the Parson's sheep as they would have been until relatively recently, but all continue to be managed by mowing in most cases. They continue to be meadows. The Victorian Parson was often interested in natural history and no doubt studied the wildlife in the nearest place to the Rectory, the churchyard. The history of the natural sciences (botany, entomology and so on) is littered with the great works of study by the Clergy. There has been a very long and fruitful connection between Christianity and the natural sciences and we seek to add something slightly different to this strand of curiosity and wonder.

These ancient meadows also hold the bones of our ancestors, metaphorically for us all and individually for families whose roots go far back into the history of their communities. For the many more rootless families who have moved and moved again, it is extraordinary to find a long lost memorial to an ancestor from two or three hundred years ago in a country churchyard. It brings to life our rural past and forebears and links us to the land. We can find the attachment to our own long past through churchyards, regardless of whether our own ancestors are there.

This link goes further than an acknowledgement of family history and can set us on a spiritual journey, placing ourselves in the cycle of life shown abundantly round us. As one generation is seen to pass to the next in the memorials we read and in the wildlife we observe, we can take comfort and hope for our own futures. The messages we read illustrate the love of others, and the faith of those buried in the promises of Christianity – of love and life after death. The glorious settings, such as for those churchyards nestled in the Downs of Sussex, and the intricate beauty of the plants and animals which inhabit many of our churchyards point to something greater than ourselves.

It would be wrong to think that churchyard meadows are only rural features. Many formerly rural churchyards are now part of the urban scene, as the villages they provided for have been swallowed up by the growth of towns and cities over the past two centuries. And not all churchyards are so ancient. Several in this book were created in the 19th century when villages were moved for one reason or another, such as St Mark's in Hadlow Down which was built in 1836. The fact that they were created at a time when the countryside was still filled with wildlife means that they too have become lifeboats, carrying their wildlife through the choppy seas of tumultuous landscape change.

Sussex is one of the richest counties in England for wildlife and nature, and is steeped in history. The Saxon influence can still be seen in place names and some buildings, while the Normans, landing in Sussex first, made their mark very early on in that conquest. Many of the churches in this survey are Norman with some evidence of Saxon still remaining. Sussex hangs onto wildflower meadows at a landscape scale, while other counties just have a handful scattered throughout their countryside. The Weald in particular still has a substantial resource of wildflower meadows, perhaps 1,000 hectares in all; around a fifth of the surviving resource in England - only Worcestershire has more.

Churchyards, ancient and modern, bring together a rich community of nature and human history, in places where the sacred and the human naturally coincide. This makes them unique. And it is this unique collision of values that we wished to investigate in our project – The Nature of God's Acre. We wanted to find out how people viewed the nature in their churchyards, and whether it affected their experiences of being in their churchyards, when there for a variety of different reasons.

Church location

Key

1 **St Leonard's** Aldrington
2 **St Philip's** Aldrington
3 **All Saints** West Dean, with St Michael and All Angels, Litlington
4 **St Michael the Archangel** Penhurst
5 **St Mary's** Barcombe
6 **St Mary the Virgin** Battle
7 **St Martin's** Westmeston
8 **St Peter** and **St Paul's** Peasmarsh
9 **St Bartholomew's** Burwash
10 **St Mark's** Hadlow Down
11 **St Margaret the Queen** Buxted
12 **St Peter's** Chailey
13 **St Giles** Dallington

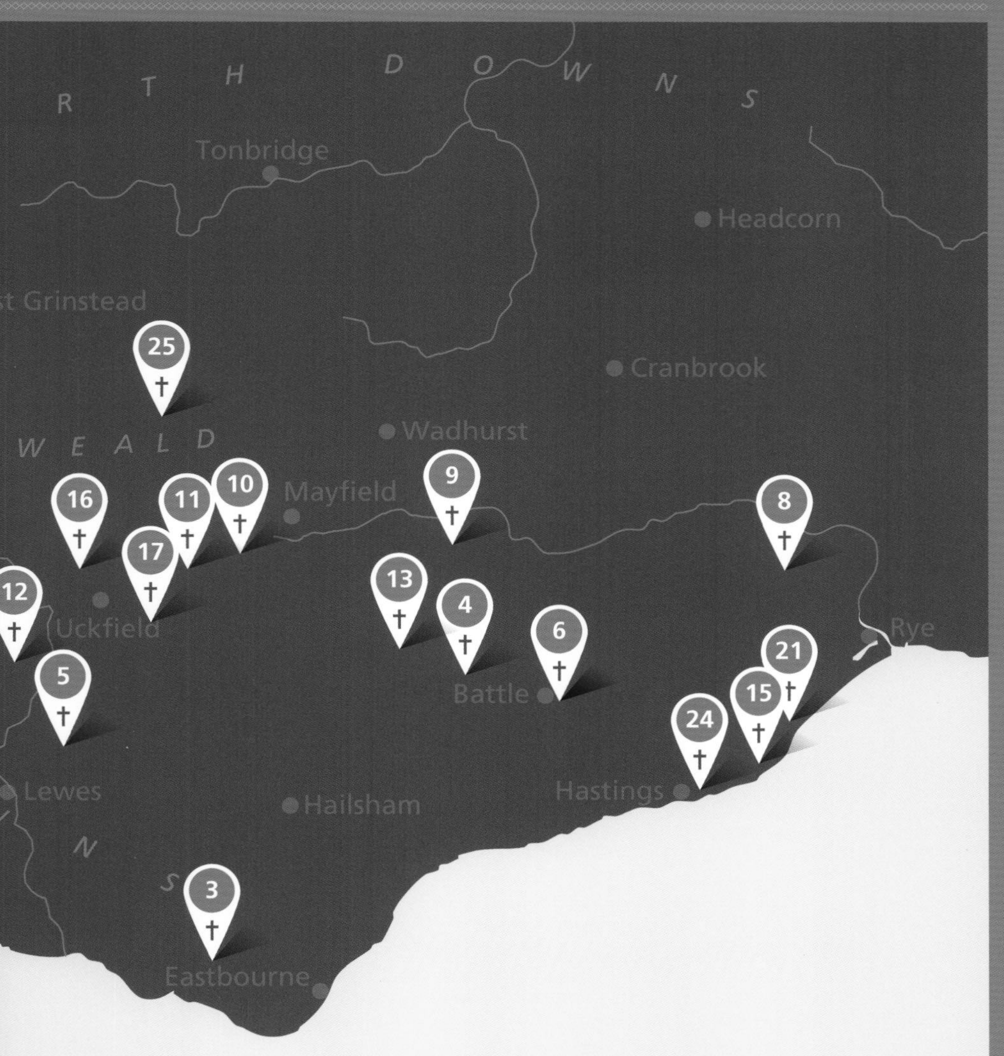

14 **St Mary the Virgin** East Preston
15 **St Andrew's** Fairlight
16 **St Andrew** and **St Mary's** Fletching
17 **St Thomas à Becket** Framfield
18 **St John the Baptist** Kirdford
19 **St Andrew** Oving
20 **All Saints** Patcham
21 **St Mary** and **St Peter's** Pett
22 **St Peter's** Terwick
23 **St Peter's** Slinfold
24 **St Clement's** Hastings
25 **St Michael and All Angels** Withyham
26 **St John's** Coolhurst

Methods

We chose 40 parishes across Sussex from the Diocese of Chichester, to include parishes from each Deanery in the Diocese. Fifteen of these parishes were chosen on account of their known or suspected value for wildlife: these included a number of Sites of Nature Conservation Interest (SNCIs), churchyards which have been identified by the Sussex Biological Records Centre as being important for their wildlife at the county level. The other 25 parishes were selected at random. This enabled us to carry out some statistical analysis on the results, allowing us to make some broader statements about churchyards in Sussex, beyond just the sample.

We contacted the Churchwardens and incumbents of each of these parishes to find out whether they were willing to take part in the project. We then devised a questionnaire (see the Appendix), which was sent to each parish. It could be completed either as a paper questionnaire or online. The survey started in late December 2013 and the last responses were received in late March 2014. We collected 175 responses from 25 parishes.

The results of the survey are considered in Part 2. For each parish that provided a response, we have prepared a churchyard summary, including information about the church and churchyard, as well as some of the responses from each parish concerning their churchyard.

Based on completed questionnaires, we also approached a small number of respondents for a more in-depth interview, either on the phone or face to face. The results of these interviews are reflected on theologically, alongside additional comments made in the survey responses.

Part 1

The Churchyard Summaries

† St Leonards'

Aldrington (BN3 4ED)

The churchyard is on the north side, at the west end of New Church Road in Hove. It is 474m² and includes a 'Secret Garden' in the north-west corner where there is a vegetable garden, bee hives and a new pond. The churchyard is a place of peace and birdsong in an urban setting.

† St Philip's

Aldrington (BN3 4BB)

The churchyard is on the north side of New Church Road, next to the small shopping area of Richardson Road. While small, it is surprisingly tranquil, with birds and insects attracted to the wildflowers and other native plants in the hedgerow and flower beds.

† All Saints

West Dean (BN25 4AL)

All Saints is a very old Norman church with traces of Saxon age stonework and an unusual squat gabled spire. The Old Parsonage next to the church is the oldest priest's house in England still in occupation. The church was extensively altered in the early 14th century.

The graveyard is small. The only part which is not in view from the front is on the north side, but a bench has been provided for contemplation. Lovely setting. Wildlife in plenty.

† St Michael

Litlington (BN26 5RD)

St. Michael the Archangel is also Norman, first built around 1150AD and then remodelled in 1863. A 13th century sundial survives on the porch and two more can be seen on the buttresses. A wooden shingled spire sits on a low tower.

Church and yard are beautifully sited in countryside; peaceful, tranquil for reflection.

The churchyard has a variety of wildflowers reflecting its location on the chalk.

When asked how wildlife affected the experience of being in the churchyard, parishioners said:

Makes me realise that I am part of nature, part of something larger than myself. I feel in awe of the scope and breadth of the world around us and grateful that I have the senses to enjoy it. I feel sad that so much of the local countryside is being eroded.

The presence of wildlife in a churchyard changes the experience from what can be quite sombre to an uplifting one. One feels God's presence in the beauty of nature.

† St Michael the Archangel

Penhurst (TN33 9QP)

In the hamlet of Penhurst, St Michael's church dates from around 1340 with substantial extension and alteration over the following one and a half centuries.

The church is built of Wealden sandstone and was renovated from a derelict state in the early 1960s by Paul Broomhall, who lived in the adjacent Manor House. He also established a trust fund for its upkeep.

When asked how the presence of wildlife affected their experience of being in the churchyard, local residents said:

Frankly, it is the peace of the location and view beyond the private burial ground, not the wildlife, that draws me to visit more often.

Nice to see the nature and wildlife.

We are fortunate that Penhurst is in a deeply rural setting, quiet & peaceful without the intrusion of noisy traffic and the rush of more urban life. The wildlife of all sorts mentioned in this survey adds to the general ambience, it cannot be manufactured.

[1] NB: St Mary's, Barcombe, is not the SNCI churchyard, but all responses came from here. St Bartholomew's is the SNCI churchyard.
[2] Power to nominate an individual to become the parish priest.
[3] L. F. Salzman (Ed) A History of the County of Sussex: Volume 7: The rape of Lewes (1940).

† St Mary's

Barcombe (BN8 5TS)[1]

The church is set some distance away from the village of Barcombe itself; following the plague in the 14th century the villagers re-built their settlement a mile from the original church. The oldest part of the church, the nave, is 12th century. The tower was constructed in the 14th century. The church was extensively altered in Victorian times.

After the Reformation the advowson[2] of Barcombe church was given to Sir Thomas Cromwell (whose life was dramatized in *Wolf Hall* and Hilary Mantel's other novels) and after his demise, to Henry VIII's fifth wife, Ann of Cleves. After that divorce the advowson returned to the Crown and is now with the Lord Chancellor.[3]

When asked how the presence of wildlife altered their experiences of being in the churchyard, parishioners said:

Nature adds a lot to my feelings of spirituality in the graveyard, because it is a beautiful reminder of creation.

It makes me feel closer to God. A spiritual moment.

God's creation is the wildlife. I prefer that to Man's creation, the gravestones, etc.

As a nature-lover, seeing wildflowers, birds, etc. around always enhances an experience.

It does not make the experience different.

Our churchyard is in a beautiful location with far reaching views; it is calm and peaceful but surrounded by working farms. Nature and life is all around, and it makes the cycle of life seem so natural, where so many people are resting, and so many generations.

Gives one a sense of human life & death being part of nature.

It is good to see living things in a place associated with death.

Impresses me with the beauty of God's world.

If there were no wildlife in the churchyard I would be less likely to visit.

Without the wildflowers the churchyard would be a bit barren, especially without the snow drops in winter.

It gives a connection with God's wider creation and deepens my spiritual life.

† St Mary the Virgin

Battle (TN33 0AN)

St Mary the Virgin, Battle, was founded in 1115 to serve the community which had grown up around the Benedictine Abbey of St Martins that was built on the site of the Battle of Hastings. There are some very fine mediaeval wall paintings and tombs, as well as crosses carved into the walls by Crusaders.

The municipal cemetery in Battle is rich in wildlife and has been made a SNCI for its flower-rich grassland, woodland and stream.

Parishioners agreed that the presence of wildlife added to their feelings of peace when visiting the churchyard.

It all adds to a feeling of oneness with the world in general and also the beauty and history of the place makes me feel at peace with myself.

...a reminder that life is a constant circle of new life and growth.

From http://www.stmarysbattle.org.uk/en/history/introduction

† St Martin's

Westmeston, Beacon Parish (BN6 8RJ)

At the foot of the South Downs, surrounded by farmland, St Martin's Westmeston was originally built just after 1100, with some further work in the 13th century. The church was then mostly rebuilt in Victorian times and little remains of the mediaeval church.

The rural church is surrounded by farmland and the churchyard is designated as a SNCI, providing an excellent example of a churchyard managed with nature and wildlife in mind. The churchyard comprises a species-rich grassland habitat, with wildflowers and scattered elder, yew and birch trees. Numerous species of bat have been found roosting in the church building itself. The churchyard was recognised for its wildlife value long ago, as part of the Living Churchyard project.

Parishioners appreciate the value of wildlife when visiting the churchyard. They said:

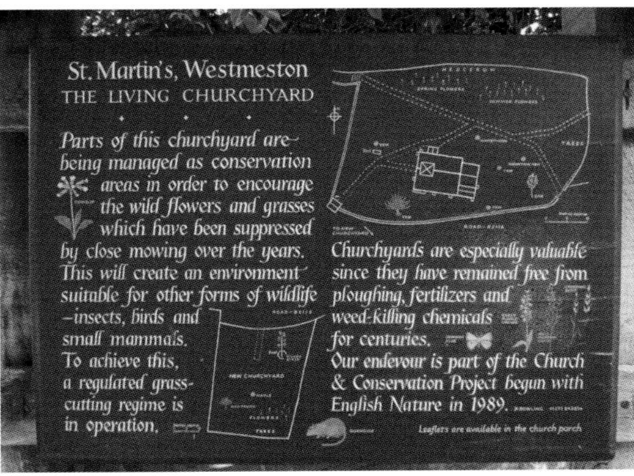

If any wildlife is there when I visit it is an added delight and adds to the joy of visiting.

A well-tended but natural churchyard with wildlife gives a sense of peace and natural order.

Most people live a busy life and increasingly the senses become overstimulted (noise, pollution, etc.). Stepping into a churchyard, like Westmeston, gives those senses a chance to relax and therefore the brain also. On entering church you are more ready to listen.

...adds to the joy of visiting the family graves.

† St Peter & Paul's

Peasmarsh, Beckley with Peasmarsh (TN31 6XE)

The Church of St Peter & St Paul's, Peasmarsh, sits on a hill with fine views over the Rother and the Tillingham valleys. In Saxon times Peasmarsh was known as Tetbald and there was an Anglo Saxon minster where the church now stands, with Roman remains indicating it may have been occupied much longer. The village now lies several hundred metres to the north of the church, possibly as a result of the Black Death.

The church of St Peter and St Paul's was built in 1070 and much still survives. The tower dates from 1170 and further alterations were made in subsequent centuries.[4]

Parishioners felt that the wildlife enhanced their experience of being in the churchyard. One mentioned the feeling of "pre-Christian spirituality" perhaps reflecting the long and ancient history of the site. Others said:

It enriches the experience.

We are fortunate to live in a very rural area where nature and natural have the same meaning. Wildlife in the churchyard is heavily indebted to the balance of nature in the much greater area of surrounding farmland.

It gives it a 'rounded' feeling of harmony. I'm happy to see the wildlife in close proximity to the dead. It reminds me of Nature's ways of recycling.

I go because the peace and contemplation are there and I go to celebrate it.

...inner peace is a very personal experience and difficult to explain.

The beauty of God's creation to the fore.

Makes one more aware of nature though, as Peasmarsh is still a rural village, the countryside is all around you if you live there. I do see more wildlife in my garden because a) I encourage wildlife and b) I spend more time in my garden than at the church.

[4] www.achurchnearyou.com

† St Bartholomew's

Burwash (TN19 7EH)

The church of St Bartholomew's dates back to around 1090, though it was enlarged in the 13th and 14th centuries, before being rebuilt in Victorian times. The Norman tower still survives. Victorian building work to lower the floor led to the churchyard being dug out around the church.[5]

Slightly more of those who responded to the survey felt there was enough wildlife in Burwash churchyard, rather than not enough. An unusual white/grey squirrel is a notable member of the churchyard wildlife.

Some parishioners felt that the presence of wildlife changed the way they experienced their churchyard. They said:

It is good to see that graves are well tended, respected and remembered.

Just part of God's beautifully created world.

The setting is naturally beautiful and the further you walk, the more distant the traffic noise on the main road. A fairly wild setting, not too manicured, is soothing and natural.

I cannot imagine the churchyard without the presence of nature.

Highlights the natural rhythm of life, tranquillity, sense of perspective...

It's an uplifting experience and echoes the circle of nature that we are all part of, which seems especially relevant in a graveyard.

It makes one start off with a sense of tranquillity and permanence.

I feel at one with nature and lucky to have such a beautiful place to visit.

When walking in our churchyard there are no visible signs of the 21st century, i.e. distraction of telecommunication aerials, dishes, vehicles, etc.

I feel I am visiting a beautiful peaceful place and feel spiritually uplifted.

It is good to feel God's presence all around us in our daily life.

[5] www.burwash.org

† St Mark's

Hadlow Down; Buxted & Hadlow Down (TN22 4HY)

Originally built in 1836, then rebuilt in Edwardian times, St Mark's has a shingled spire and this stunning stone-built church is a Grade II listed building, recognised for its historical importance and impressive Gothic Revival architecture.

The churchyard contains several official war graves from the First and Second World Wars and in commemoration of the Queen's Silver Jubilee, a Jubilee Gate was erected at the entrance.[6]

As a SNCI, the churchyard contains a remarkable number of grassland plant species, along with spotted orchids and some green-winged orchids. This churchyard is managed sympathetically for its wildlife and for visitors: a large part of the area is allowed to grow as meadow each summer but with mowed walkways to allow access to graves. It is part of the National Living Churchyard nature reserve network.

The local community values the wildlife of the churchyard, one resident remarked:

The sound of our churchyard in the summer is wonderful.

When asked how the presence of wildlife changed the way they felt when in the churchyard, one said:

I just enjoy being there. It is sympathetically cared for, with paths carefully cut, leaving long grass with its wildflowers in the majority of the churchyard. We have a wonderful selection of wildflowers in the appropriate seasons.

[6] www.bhdchurches.org.uk/historymark.htm

† St Margaret the Queen

Buxted; Buxted & Hadlow Down (TN22 4HY)

The 13th century church of St Margaret the Queen sits within the ancient Buxted Park. The church was built in the same year (1250) as St Margaret the Queen of Scotland was canonised. The churchyard is exceptionally old and a yew tree there has been estimated to be over 2,000 years old.[7]

The churchyard holds a number of interesting graves, including William Wordsworth's brother, who was the Rector of St Margaret, and the author Winston Graham who wrote the Poldark novels. Buxted Park is a nationally important site for wildlife and history. Its ancient trees support rare insects while the wildlife-rich grassland is important for its fungi.

St Margaret's churchyard elicits mixed feelings from its parishioners. A few felt that a churchyard should be tidy and that the lichen should be cleaned from the gravestones. The majority felt that the churchyard should be mown less to allow the wildlife to thrive.

Others viewed the churchyard within a landscape rich in wildlife (the surrounding park) and felt that churchyards should be kept tidy.

I love all aspects of wildlife but feel there is plenty of countryside without the use of graveyards. It used to be cut and tidy and got lots of comments from visitors.

A churchyard is for respect and a tidy, well-kept churchyard is a credit to the parish.

When asked to consider how they value wildlife when visiting their churchyard, people said:

Being glad to be alive and grateful to God for all fauna and flora that enrich that. For the thoughts that are generated by watching evidence of the seasons, renewal and beauty.

I am not that conscious of the wildlife in the churchyard – pleasant yes, but no more.

It's more natural and a nice counterbalance to 'sanitised' areas. It feels a privilege to enjoy God's natural environment, which is declining.

Wildlife in the churchyard shows the beauty of God's creation, that the cycle of life continues & is forever renewing itself. It reminds me of Christ's resurrection and God's promise of everlasting life to all who believe in him.

One has only to contrast it with the thought of a barren and regimented graveyard to appreciate how enormously the rural, partly wild, environment transforms into a peaceful and calming place.

Some parts of the churchyard should be 'tidy', but not all of it.

[7] www.ancient-yew.org/treeInfo.php?link=316

† St Peter's

Chailey (BN8 4DA)

The name Chailey may derive from the Saxon for 'cuckoo meadow'. Another possibility is broom or gorse meadow, from 'Chag Leah'. Chailey may be the longest parish in Britain, at seven miles long. St Peter's, Chailey, is a 13th century church.[8]

The churchyard at St Peter's is exceptionally rich in wildflowers. As a SNCI, this churchyards' flowers include dropwort, pepper-saxifrage and marjoram. There are also several ancient yew trees near the church. Hawthorn, elder, hazel and ash, along with mixed hedges, provide an excellent habitat for birds and other species.

Asked how the presence of wildlife changed their experience of being in the churchyard, parishioners said:

Flowers and birds complement the spiritual experience.

Presence of wildlife shows peace and calm, this in turn reflects on one's mood.

Evidence of God's creation and our part in it.

I like to sit in the churchyard for thought and contemplation. I enjoy the churchyard as I feel that I am not alone, although I am. I like to watch the wildlife as it lives on and it just confirms that life goes on even after death.

Feeling of continuity.

Enhances the preciousness and wonder of life.

Nature helps, in my view, reflection and contemplation – to feel part of a wider world, beyond our offices and kitchens. But "improving nature" should not lead to wild untended gardens, without respect for the graves, which should be well tended. There is a balance.

It brings a sense of perspective to one's life.

The green environment is refreshing…even with the traffic noise in the distance.

All nature seems to be in decline. The churchyard is one area that has abundant wildlife and this gives a positive, relaxed feeling. The beauty of bird song is particularly uplifting and enhances one's time in the churchyard.

Memory of loved one's love of animals. A feeling of peace and fellowship.

[8] From www.stpeterchailey.org

† St Giles

Dallington (TN21 9NH)

Dallington church is Victorian, the original church having been replaced in 1864. Just the tower and unusual stone spire remain from the original church. The churchyard is very old.

The nearby Sugar Loaf Folly was built by ('Mad') Jack Fuller to resemble Dallington church tower in Sussex. He had made a bet that he could see the spire of St Giles from his manor house at Brightling, but when he realised this was untrue he had workmen erect this folly in order to win the bet.[9]

When we asked parishioners how the presence of wildlife changes their experience of being in the churchyard, they said:

Adds to country life.

Daughter & mother buried here; they loved wildlife, birds and butterflies. So I feel much happier when these are in evidence when I visit them. Plus I consider it to be very important to encourage wildflowers, etc.

The churchyard is for all God's creatures, not just man and moles. Being closer to wildlife is closer to God in the churchyard than the church, where one is closer to Man's interpretation of God.

Having wildlife around makes life worthwhile and pleasurable.

It's a churchyard, not a cemetery. It's warm, not cold and austere. Time doesn't seem to matter.

[9] http://johnmadjackfuller.homestead.com/Sugarloaf.html

† St Mary the Virgin

East Preston (BN16 2SP)

The parish church, St Mary the Virgin, is of Norman origin, built around the 12th century, and is built on the ancient Saxon burial ground.[10]

The churchyard or litten may well have been a Saxon burial ground before the church was built, or before the present Norman church was founded. Littens are often about three quarters of an acre in area, as is East Preston. This is because the 'customary acre', as derived from the common field strips, was less than a statute acre. The name 'church acre' is quite apt. The ancient boundaries still survive as flint walls on two sides, but the elms that marked the other two sides were lost to Dutch Elm Disease.

The litten was managed as meadow or pasture before the advent of headstones. In 1579 it was reported that: "Our Vicar doth sometimes put both oxen and kyne into the churchyard."

As the parish has grown, the churchyard has been extended several times up until recent years.[11]

When asked how wildlife changed their experience of the churchyards, parishioners said:

I like all the flowers and wildlife as it's calming, and can make a very sad place seem more happy.

If I were to take a moment from the monthly 'churchyard clearing' duty to sit on one of the few benches provided, it might be good to observe the wildlife around – but I actually find the gravestones and the epitaphs of more interest than the wildlife.

It's good to see birds, etc. enjoying the graveyard and just to stop and listen to their singing makes me feel good.

I feel close to the deceased.

[10] http://www.eastprestonvillage.co.uk/history.php
[11] http://eastpreston.inthepast.org.uk/ep_church.htm
[12] www.fairlightandpett.com
[13] http://www.roughwood.net/ChurchAlbum/EastSussex/Fletching/FletchingChurch2005.htm

† St Andrew's

Fairlight (TN35 4AB)

There was already a church in Fairlight at the time the Doomsday Book was written. This was replaced in 1180 and this church lasted until 1845 when it in turn was replaced.[12] A 14th century bell still resides in the belfry.

The graveyard is very old and includes the parents and sister of Cecil Rhodes, the founder of Rhodesia (now Zimbabwe). Richard D'Oyly Carte, who founded the company which originally staged the Gilbert and Sullivan operas, is also buried here.

† St Andrew & St Mary

Fletching (TN22 3SS)

The church of St Andrew and St Mary in Fletching is very old, showing traces of late Saxon and early Norman stonework[13], with the current church completed around 1230. Restoration took place in the 1880s. The spire was first erected in 1340.

One parishioner explained how wildlife in the churchyard made them feel:

...more connected to God and his universe; a reminder of how precious the natural world is to humans and how we must care for it.

For another, the churchyard reminded her of her late husband:

...of happy times while husband was vicar at church – all too briefly. Had great enjoyment of country (especially birds) after many years in London.

For others, when asked, the presence of wildlife did not enhance their experiences of the churchyard:

It does not. I expect the churchyard to be a peaceful place.

St Thomas à Becket

Framfield (TN22 5NH)

Framfield is an ancient parish, perhaps dating back to the 7th century. There was a Saxon church here before the Norman church was built around 1200, just after Thomas Becket was martyred and canonised.

The churchyard is rich in wildlife – a recent survey found 120 species of wildflowers, grasses, shrubs and trees, while butterflies, damselflies and slow-worms abound. Six bird boxes have been erected in the trees around the churchyard. A churchyard management plan[14] has been written by local resident and ecologist, Sally Clifton. Sally notes: "The challenge is to maintain the right balance between keeping paths accessible to visitors, whilst taking care of the best of the wild flora allowing them to flower so beautifully in spring or summer, depending on the species, and to set seed before being mown or strimmed at the best time."

Asked how wildlife made their experiences of being in the churchyard different, parishioners said:

Seeing wildlife in the churchyard (or anywhere) reminds me of how God cares about every tiny detail of his creation and our lives; how he loves beauty; how he sustains his creation and makes things work together harmoniously.

One visitor spoke of the wildlife and nature in the churchyard:

It seems to bring you closer to the natural world and so closer to God.

Adds so much more depth to it.

To be at one with God's creation.

It is comforting to see nature thriving in such a special place.

It enriches the experience.

You can be alone, away from noise and other distractions, and not feel isolated and 'lonely'. Wildflowers (celandines today!), birds/birdsong and butterflies can give hope and lift your spirits, a sign of life.

A wonderful place.

Peacefulness helps my concentration.

[14] http://www.framfieldchurch.org.uk/churchyardplan.html

† St John the Baptist

Kirdford (RH14 0LT)

A Grade 1 listed building on the southern side of Kirdford, St John the Baptist church is located within the Kirdford Conservation Area, the oldest part of the village. The church was likely first built around 1100, reflected by the Saxon-type masonry in evidence.

The churchyard is a SNCI and, as such, is home to a wonderful variety of wildlife in a natural grassland and meadow habitat. This has created an unusual woodland meadow flora with meadow flowers, such as ox-eye daisy, hoary plantain, common knapweed and burnet saxifrage, alongside species more typical of open woodland glades, such as early purple orchids and wild daffodil. Recent records indicate that adders, now quite uncommon, are living in the churchyard.

Most parishioners agreed that the presence of wildlife changed the way they felt when in the churchyard. They said:

It gives me a feeling of continuity that all living things are born, grow, flower and finally rest in peace amongst the beauty of nature in God's creation. I think back to our ancestors who have worshipped, lived, loved, raised families, died for our country.

...the right sort of setting is more conducive to anything you would wish to do or would wish to feel in a religious place.

Because it feels part of the countryside as well as sacred ground.

...happy memories of watching wildlife in the past with loved ones.

A churchyard takes me away from the traffic (human and mechanical) of life beyond its walls. As a country person I enjoy sharing my time with other areas of God's own creation.

One person felt that the "main area is very well kept. The lower area called the 'conservation area' is a disgrace, totally overgrown with brambles and ant hills", which illustrates the careful balance needed in managing these areas – creating a balance between encouraging special and rare wildlife and enabling access to the graves of loved ones.

† St Andrew

Oving (PO20 2DE)

St Andrew is a 13th century church with an unusual wooden shingle spire. The spire has a golden cockerel weathervane. The church was founded in 1220 and from the outside little has changed, while the interior was extensively restored by the Victorians in the 1860s. There is a churchyard and a separate graveyard 200m to the north.[15]

When asked how the presence of wildlife in their churchyard made them feel when visiting it, parishioners said:

The calm and tranquillity of the surroundings is definitely enhanced by the sound of birds and the beauty of wildflowers.

The more wildlife there is, the longer I would be likely to linger in the churchyard to enjoy the peace and quiet.

Good to be alive.

They link us to the wonders of God's world. Nature shows his great love for us all.

Contemplation of the vast variety of God's creation and how humble and thankful it makes me feel.

Photo by Stephen Bennett

[15] http://www.ovingcommunity.org.uk/church.php

† All Saints

Patcham (BN1 8YE)

All Saints dates back to the 12th century and an unusual survivor is a 13th century wall painting of the Apocalypse which was rediscovered in 1883.[16] There was at least one previous church, which was mentioned in the Doomsday Book.

In the churchyard is the grave of Daniel Scales, a smuggler shot by Customs' men in November 1796.[17] The inscription states:

OF DANIEL SCALES, WHO WAS UNFORTUNATELY SHOT ON THURSDAY EVENING, NOV. 7TH, 1796.

Alas! swift flew the fatal lead,
Which pierced through the young man's head.
He instant fell, resigned his breath,
And closed his languid eyes in death.
All you who do this stone draw near,
Oh! pray let fall the pitying tear.
From this sad instance may we all
Prepare to meet Jehovah's call.

Some parishioners agreed that the presence of wildlife added to the experience of visiting the churchyard:

It enhances the feeling that the churchyard engenders a spiritual feeling.

Others felt that the churchyard needed more management:

We are all part of God's wonderful creation. Local council is responsible for maintaining the cutting, but due to lack of funds this means work that should be done is not, in spite of repeated reminders.

Photo by Tony Mould

[16] www.sites.google.com/allsaintspatcham

[17] Mybrightonandhove.org.uk

† St Mary & St Peter

Pett (TN35 4HE)

There are records for a church at Pett from the 13th century. The present church was built in 1864. This church is a prominent feature in the landscape, with a 75ft tall spire.[18]

There are some very old memorials in the churchyard, dating back to mediaeval times. While the church has been rebuilt, the churchyard remains as it is.

The churchyard supports reptiles such as slow-worms and common lizards.

A local resident said that the presence of wildlife in the churchyard when visiting the graves of a loved one made the experience "more meaningful". Some felt that the churchyard had "too many trees and invasive vegetation", such as bramble and ivy.

† St Peter

Terwick, Terwick with Rotate (GU31 5EQ)

The tiny church of St Peter, Terwick, stands on its own in fields next to the old Midhurst Road. It was originally built in the 12th, perhaps 11th, century. In the churchyard, to the west of the church, is an ancient churchyard cross and a small yew tree.

In 2013, to commemorate the Diamond Jubilee, two elm saplings, grown from stock resistant to Dutch Elm Disease, were planted in the churchyard to replace those lost when the disease swept through England in the early 1970s.

Many visitors to this peaceful village churchyard felt that the presence of wildlife helped to enhance their experience:

It helps one to identify with the natural world which has evolved slowly over the millennia and for a moment or two leave behind the pressures, distractions and distortions of modern life, which progresses at breakneck speed.

Wildlife is part of God's creation, which will hopefully continue this way into the future.

I like to feel part of the whole creation and in tune with the wildlife.

Wildlife enhances the environment of the churchyard.

It makes it a very peaceful place to visit.

† St Peter's

Slinfold (RH13 0QU)

St Peter's was built in the late 11th or early 12th century. A timber steeple was constructed in the 16th century. This church was mostly replaced in 1861. Archaeological investigations hint at the presence of a high status Roman building on or near the site of the church.

When asked how the presence of wildlife changed the experience of being in the churchyard, parishioners' views included the following:

Being aware of the richness of God's creation adds awe to the contemplative state.

Makes it feel more natural, that you are in tune with the country.

It enhances it. The churchyard has many beds of roses, etc., but also much 'wildlife'. Together they greatly enhance the experience and the churchyard is well maintained and open to all at all times.

Nature is part of God's creation and we sometimes need to be reminded of that.

[18] www.fairlightandpett.com

† St Clements

Hastings (TN34 3EW)

The church of St Clements is one of two ancient churches (the other is All Saints) that form the Old Town Parish of Hastings. St Clements can trace its origins back to 1080AD although it was ravaged by the French in 1339, and again in 1377, and was rebuilt in 1380.

It has many interesting features including a 15th century font depicting the Passion of Christ and two magnificent chandeliers – one of which was presented by the Hastings Barons of the Cinque Ports who raised the funds for the purchase by selling the canopy and silver staves held above George III at his coronation in 1761. The other chandelier was purchased by the Townsmen of Hastings.

St Clements has two beautiful East End stained glass windows – the work of Philip Cole – which replaced the original windows blown out by a bomb blast in the Second World War when a German bomb demolished the Old Swann Inn in the High Street dating back to 1309.[19]

Dante Gabriel Rossetti, poet and artist, married Elizabeth Siddall in St Clements in 1860.

When asked how wildlife changed the way they felt when in the churchyard for other reasons, parishioners gave the following views:

...a living place and not just a relic of the past.

...the beauty of creation."

One commented on a more practical issue:

Seagulls are a problem. Many visitors lose their fish & chips.

[19] http://www.achurchnearyou.com/hastings-st-clement/

† St Michael & All Angels

Withyham (TN7 4BD)

There has certainly been a church at Withyham since a very early period. It is mentioned in 1291 in connection with Edward I sending money to Pope Nicholas IV for a crusade and Withyham was then valued at 45 marks.

The church was apparently almost completely rebuilt in the 14th century and consisted of a nave with a north and south aisle, chancel and west tower and at the east end of the north aisle was the chapel of the Sackville family.

On 16th June 1663 the church was struck by lightning coming in at the steeple, melting the bells, and up to the chancel where it smashed the monuments to the Sackville family to pieces.

The rebuilding of the church finished around 1672 and the Sackville Chapel was not completed until 1680. The church was subsequently extensively remodelled by the Victorians.

The ashes of the famous English gardener Vita Sackville-West are entombed in the Sackville family vault in an inkpot.[20]

Bats, frogs, deer, foxes and badgers make use of the churchyard and a recent survey also found yellow-necked mice and toads.

When asked how wildlife changed the way they felt when visiting their churchyard for other reasons, parishioners felt it enhanced their experiences and made the following comments:

Any visit to a church is made more meaningful in attractive surroundings.

For me it is easier to be nearer God's presence in a country churchyard, it is lovely to stop and watch animals.

The peaceful moment is enhanced by good housekeeping, tree management, the protection and awareness of rare species and care for God's acre. Enhances community spirit.

[20] www.withyhamchurch.org

† St John the Evangelist

Coolhurst (RH13 6PJ)

St John, Coolhurst, is situated in beautiful woodland belonging to the Coolhurst Estate. It was built by Charles Scrase-Dickins of Coolhurst and consecrated in 1839.

Much of the interior woodwork was made from trees grown on the Coolhurst estate. There is a private burial area to the west of the church owned and maintained by the Coolhurst Estate.

The Horsham stone for the roof came from a blacksmith's shop in Slaugham which was demolished in 1837 and extensive restoration of the roof was undertaken in 1975. This roof currently hosts interesting species of mosses and the surrounding burial ground is a haven for wildflowers.

Although St John's was not part of our original survey we have been allowed to reproduce this personal reflection by a member of the congregation about the churchyard:

In April 2010 my husband Mike was laid to rest in the ashes plot at St. John, Coolhurst. It was a warm April afternoon when his ashes were committed to the ground in a simple but very moving service. I have over the last four years visited the churchyard on many occasions to tend his plot and lay flowers for birthdays and anniversaries.

St. John's churchyard is a very special place, standing as it does in its quiet spot amongst the trees of the Coolhurst Estate. The ashes plot is situated to the right of the vestry in the sunniest spot. It has the sun all day on those days when the sun is shining. When I am there on those sunny days I sit for a while on the step by the vestry door and listen to the birds, feeling the sun on my face. I cannot be unhappy in such a glorious location, a tranquil place for quiet reflection.

I sometimes look around the other graves reading the names and wondering what the people named were like. There are some that have a large and small gravestone marking where there is an adult and child buried together. The history of these people still lives on in those who knew them. When my time comes I will join Mike and we will spend eternity together in our sunny spot. Others will come and tend the plots and perhaps take a moment to consider who we were and what we might have done with our lives.

Part 2

The Survey Results

The Nature of God's Acre: A theological reflection by Mark Betson

I'm glad we have a very long walk through the churchyard as in that five minutes my wife and I experience a great sense of peace.

As part of this study we included some final questions on the survey that was sent to the selected churches which asked, firstly: Do you value the presence of wildlife when visiting the churchyard for contemplation or visiting the grave of a loved one? And then if 'yes' to this question, the survey asked: How does this make the experience different? The respondent had space to record their thoughts. Finally, the survey ended by asking if the respondent would be willing to be interviewed at a later date. This information, capturing peoples' thoughts and feelings in their own words, revealed another insight into the data collected. In this chapter I have reflected theologically on these comments and put into words some of the ideas we have encountered.

The Churchyard

Churchyards are special places. They are not like other green spaces. They are not the same as fields, gardens, parks or woods – special though they can be. They are places where life, death and rebirth meet and have met for centuries. Unlike the cycle of life played out before us in the flora and fauna of other habitats, in churchyards we are actively part of that cycle marked out by the names on the memorials of past generations.

Perhaps surprisingly in this place where mortality is very clearly defined, in all of the conversations we had with people who spend time in churchyards there is not a hint of sadness in their experience. Overridingly, the sensation reflected back to us is one of peace, tranquility and comfort. Their experience is also not solely one of the past but also something which has meaning to their present. As Peter Stanford comments at the end of his book *How to Read a Graveyard: Journeys in the Company of the Dead* (a book which came out of his visits to a local graveyard whilst walking his dog):

But we don't have to limit ourselves to social studies or historical investigation when in the company of the dead on a visit to a cemetery...I plan to keep on visiting, first of all for the dog – that is certainly what I tell the children – but really for me, for that reassuring sense my walks give me that I am part of a human chain, going through the cycle of birth and death as those who came before, and will come after me.[21]

Something more than the reassurance spoken of by Peter Stanford is perhaps voiced at the conclusion of the first episode of the BBC television series *Pagans and Pilgrims: Britain's Holiest Places*, where one of the reasons why people come to remains of the past is to recover something that they have lost.[22]

[21] Peter Stanford, How to read a Graveyard: Journeys in the company of the dead , p.241.
[22] Pagans and Pilgrims: Britain's Holiest Places BBC Four accessed on 19th January 2014. http://www.bbc.co.uk/programmes/b01r6z2d

From the Christian heritage of these holy places it can be argued that what is present is a sense of hope borne in the belief of those buried there in the Christian message – that death is not the final chapter and that love endures through the resurrection of Jesus Christ.[23] Even for those who are not Christian, the bonds of love and kinship demonstrated in the memorials present generate a positive reaction. In addition to the bonds between generations, these places also bind people intimately with a location – in this place they find their rest. It is possible that for these reasons people find comfort and peace in churchyards. They offer hope and connection with people and places, things which remain stable in an increasingly busy world.

But the churchyard is a 'green space' too and intrinsically part of it is the soil under which people are buried and the plants that grow in that soil. So, given the special experience they give to those who visit them, what is the relationship between the nature present in the churchyard and peoples' experience of it? It is helpful, in starting to ask this question theologically, to look back at where our churchyards have come from.

The History of the Churchyard

The history of churchyards in England begins with the arrival of Christianity to the British Isles from the Celtic missionaries of Ireland and the arrival of Augustine from Rome. With these came the founding of places of worship and prayer, places significant for the meeting of the faithful.

In selecting sacred sites, Celtic Christianity considered both practical and spiritual factors. Places were sought out where for some reason the boundaries between heaven and earth were perceived to be closer together. Some of these were traditional places from pre-Christian times such as woodlands or wells, or at burial sites where by their very nature the boundary between the material world and the spiritual world were brought close.[24] Celtic Christians were heavily influenced by kinship relations where ancestry and links to a particular place were important.[25] For the Celtic tradition the marking out of these sacred sites was impo rtant. Usually a wall was erected around them, defining the land within as holy ground and within the Christian tradition. Here the faithful were to be buried.

The wave of Christianization which accompanied the arrival of Pope Gregory I's emissary, Augustine, saw a progressive conversion of the sites of pagan shrines into churches, placing the Church in the commonly rural areas these shrines inhabited.[26] Subsequent to Augustine his later successor, Archbishop Theodore, is credited with the beginnings of the parish system where medieval landowners were encouraged to erect churches on their estates and were granted the rights of perpetual patronage.[27] These estate churches progressively developed into parish churches because of increasing rural settlement in the early medieval period following the Norman invasion.[28] The height of church building came in the period between 1150 and 1250, with a survey in 1291 indicating that there were then over 8,000 parishes.

[23] 1 Corinthians 13: 8-13, 15: 3-23.
[24] P. Sheldrake, Living Between Worlds: place and journey in Celtic spirituality (London, 1995), p.30.
[25] Ibid., p.35.
[26] N. Cooper, 'The history of English churchyard landscapes illustrated by Rivenhall Essex' in G. Pungetti, G. Oviedo and D. Hook (Eds) Sacred Species and Sites: Advances in Biocultural Conservation (Cambridge, 2012), p.98.
[27] A. Russell, The Country Parish (London: SPCK, 1986), p.190.
[28] Ibid., p.190-191.

Some of the sites selected for churches would have therefore been based on natural beauty and significant natural features, such as the Celtic tradition of seeking places in the wilderness, and the conversion of pagan sites of worship, which included yew trees, wells and springs.[29] Most however followed ancient settlement patterns and were carved out where the largely rural population were living at the time.

One of the greatest upheavals in the life of the English Church was the Reformation, beginning under Henry VIII. At its beginning the main difference to village churches was the change from ecclesiastical to secular authority by the local landowner. However, following the publication of Cranmer's *Book of Common Prayer* in 1549 and its subsequent institution, a hitherto unknown uniformity of worship was imposed on the whole Church. The effect on even the most rural church was most notable.[30] Here a type of medieval spirituality had been practised which often included a cult of prayers for the dead, the banning of which would have had a deep impact on the people there.[31]

Despite this the community spirituality, the folk religion, of particular places persisted through the Reformation and emerged following the restitution of the Stuart monarchy. Churchyards provided a focus for that spirituality and have continued to do so, forming a spiritual home for the community who have an interest in the churchyard – probably more so than the church over the years – as their forebears have a permanent space and monument there. As Nigel Cooper notes in his history of English churchyard landscapes:

There is a sense in which ancestor worship is alive and well in the English countryside: come a Sunday, probably more people will visit graves in the churchyard than will enter the church building for an official service...Villagers will often visit several relatives' graves, going back at least two generations. They will expect to follow their parents in due course, some even bothering to reserve plots to be near relatives. It brings a mindset quite different to that of the cosmopolitan person if one knows where one is to be buried.

Churchyards Today

In more recent times the situation has changed, with first an influx of people to the cities during the Industrial Revolution and now a movement back to the countryside, following a perceived better quality of living. Both of these migrations have led to the disruption of existing communities and the forming of new ones, perhaps with the graveyard being the only monument to the old community still existing. The interest acquired through generations of family being buried in the churchyard will not be shared by those newly moving into parishes and, understandably, there are tensions that can develop. These tensions exist on a number of levels and are also expressed in personal belief. A spirituality formed through long association with the churchyard and the tending of loved ones' graves will be different from one experiencing this sacred space for the first time. Incomers to parishes may not relate to the churchyard at all, particularly with declines in church membership and with them not having the investment of a loved one buried there. In cases like these Nigel Cooper laments:

[29]Cooper, 'The history of English churchyard landscapes illustrated by Rivenhall Essex', p.98
[30]E. Duffy, The Voices of Morebath: Reformation and rebellion in an English Village (London, 2001), p.128.
[31]Russell, The Country Parish, pp.197-8

Churchyards naturally receive all sorts of projections about death. In some villages death seems to have overcome the local community. This may be where there are a disproportionate number of incomers who are not relating to their new community, or the village population is just ageing and shrinking. Here nearly all care for the churchyard, apart from a few graves, has been abandoned, and the grasslands tumbling down to scrub.

However, where there is an active interest in the churchyard, by both long term members of the community and incomers alike, the management of the grassland and trees that constitute the nature of the churchyard generates strong emotions, which arise out of strongly held beliefs about these spaces. It seems that the nature of a churchyard has a strong effect on the feelings of people and the positive qualities that it reflects.

The apparent effort of a closely mown churchyard demonstrates to some that the space is cared for, that their future final rest in this place is secure, and that they will not be forgotten amongst the weeds. For others the rich abundance of wildflowers is a symbol of the Creator at work and for Christians this is also an affirmation of their faith and ultimately of the promises of eternal life.

The Ordinary Theology of Churchyard Visitors

Theology is putting into words what goes into our religious faith and practice. In this sense what takes place in theology departments in institutes and universities is secondary. Theology happens whenever someone takes time to think about what they believe and their practices surrounding issues of faith. Ordinary Theology has been developed as a concept by Jeff Astley to look at these popular theological perceptions:

Ordinary Christian Theology is my phrase for the theology and theologizing of Christians who have received little or no theological education of a scholarly, academic or systematic kind. 'Ordinary' in this context implies non-scholarly and non-academic; it fits the dictionary definition that refers to an 'ordinary person' as who is without exceptional experience or expert knowledge.[32]

Astley argues that to engage with this theology requires both empirical study, gathering information from people, and theological reflection and that is what we have attempted in this study.

Some of the empirical information collected has been analyzed by Miles King and his results are presented in the following section. In this chapter I have been informed by the empirical evidence contained in the responses to the last questions in the survey, and through subsequent interviews with some of the respondents. I endeavour to reflect theologically on what this information tells us about the spiritual relationship people have with nature in churchyards.

[32] J. Astley, Ordinary Theology (Aldershot, 2002), p.56.

For most of the respondents to the survey the presence of nature significantly enhanced the experience they had when visiting the churchyard. Here are some of the comments we had reflecting this:

The more wildlife there is, the longer I would be likely to linger in the churchyard to enjoy the peace and quiet.

Seeing wildlife in the churchyard (or anywhere) reminds me how God cares about every tiny detail of his Creation and our lives; how he loves beauty; how he sustains his Creation and makes things work together harmoniously; the reliability of the changing seasons, etc.

Wildlife in the churchyard shows the beauty of God's Creation, that the cycle of life continues and is forever renewing itself. It reminds me of Christ's resurrection and God's promise of everlasting life to all who believe in him.

The presence of wildlife in a churchyard changes the experience from what can be quite sombre to an uplifting one. One feels God's presence in the beauty of nature.

Usually I'm far too busy to be able to enjoy the experience for very long, but any evidence of wildlife could only enhance it.

How could we be living on a beautiful world without there being a mind behind it? Sensing God's enjoyment of what God has created and that he wants people to enjoy it.

Makes me realise that I am part of nature, part of something larger than myself. I feel in awe of the scope and breadth of the world around us and grateful that I have the senses to enjoy it.

But not all comments were positive about the enhancement nature provided to the churchyard. These comments indicate the ambivalence of some towards it:

Frankly it is the peace of the location and the view beyond the private burial ground, not the wildlife, that draws me to visit more often.

I love all aspects of wildlife but feel there is plenty of countryside without the use of graveyards. It used to be cut and tidy and got lots of comments from visitors.

If I were to take a moment from the monthly "churchyard clearing" duty to sit on one of the few benches provided, it might be good to observe the wildlife around – but I actually find the gravestones and the epitaphs of more interest than the wildlife.

I am not that conscious of the wildlife in the churchyard – pleasant yes, but no more.

One person in particular found the situation in their churchyard intolerable:

The main area is very well kept. The lower area called the 'conservation area' is a disgrace, totally overgrown with brambles and ant hills. It's disgusting – there have been snowdrops in the sign of a cross which have been coming up for over a 100 years and now they are covered in brambles.

However most comments were positive to having the presence of wildlife in churchyards, the caveat, illustrated in the comment above, is where nature overwhelms the monuments and graves.

There is also more depth to the experience as the churchyard is also a place set apart from the rest of the world as these comments show:

It helps one to identify with the natural world which has evolved slowly over the millennia and for a moment or two leave behind the pressures, distractions and distortions of modern life which progresses at breakneck speed.

When walking in our churchyard there are no visible signs of the 21st century, i.e. distraction of telecommunication aerials, dishes, vehicles, etc.

You can be alone, away from noise and other distractions and not feel isolated and 'lonely'. Wildflowers (celandines today!), birds/birdsong and butterflies can give hope and lift your spirits, a sign of life.

As mentioned above, churchyards receive our reflections about death and nature plays a part in these reflections:

It gives it a 'rounded' feeling of harmony. I'm happy to see the wildlife in close proximity to the dead. It reminds me of Nature's ways of recycling.

I like to sit in the churchyard for thought and contemplation. I enjoy the churchyard as I feel that I am not alone, although I am. I like to watch the wildlife as it lives on and it just confirms that life goes on even after death.

Both myself and my husband, who is not a churchgoer, want to end up here – there is something peaceful about this place, it's a typical rural churchyard. There is nothing commercial here – unlike some crematoria I have been to.

"Reminds me of happy times while my husband was vicar at church – all too briefly. Had great enjoyment of country (especially birds) after many years in London.

Daughter and mother buried here, they loved wildlife, birds and butterflies. So I feel much happier when these are in evidence when I visit them.

It is also a place which inspires people to debate issues of faith, as this comment tells us:

The churchyard is for all God's creatures, not just man and moles. Being closer to wildlife is closer to God in the churchyard than the church, where one is closer to Man's interpretation of God.

There were a few comments similarly rejecting 'church' or 'religion' but, as indicated by the survey results, most of the people who responded were committed churchgoers.

Final Reflection

Graveyards are one of the few places people feel they can come and contemplate death. Death is something we find hard to come to terms with today, much more so than in our Victorian past for example, where preparation for death was very much the business of one's later life.

As our survey and interviews have revealed, people do not find graveyards places of sadness but rather associate them with peace and comfort. This is in part because these places are set apart from the rest of the world and the busyness outside does not seem to penetrate in. They are places where time is not measured in minutes and hours but in years, decades and centuries.

However, as Nigel Cooper points out, they also receive our projections about death. They mark out continuity with past generations, whose presence gives us confidence that we too will be marked and remembered in time. This is part of the Christian message of hope that is at the heart of the origin of churchyards.

But what part does nature play in our projections about death? For many of the people we have had feedback from it is twofold: firstly, it is about new life and, secondly, it is about confidence in something beyond ourselves. The ongoing cycle of life (as commented on by a number of people) is witnessed by the nature present and gives hope that as one generation passes another is being born. Life goes on. In addition many people remarked that observing the multi-faceted and intricate parts of the plants and animals present in our churchyards points to something greater than ourselves. For some the same pointers come not from the small but the grand, particularly for our rural churchyards, where the magnificence of the setting generates a sense of awe and wonder.

The views expressed about the nature in churchyards are not universal however and tensions arise. For some a carefully tended churchyard is symbolized by closely cut grass and clean monuments, which enable easy access for loved ones and allow names on the stones to be easily read. This is not a dislike of nature but a belief that the churchyard is about people, those buried there now and for those who would like it to be their final resting place. These views come into conflict with those who then take comfort and hope from the illustration of new life and something greater than Man in the variety and interaction of wild grassland. For them the churchyard is as much about nature as people, where humanity is one facet in the greater cycle of life.

In these tensions though there is an overriding priority located in the origin of churchyards. Churchyards have been set apart from the beginning as sacred ground with the intention that the Divine is given priority in this place. In the end, churchyards do not give priority to people or to nature, but to God. They are places where those who have died are entrusted to God's care and where we have the opportunity to come and take hope and comfort in that belief. How we tend and care for these places reflects our faith in that belief. If we try to control them too closely, allowing only human influence to be reflected, then there may be no room for God. Likewise, if we turn them over entirely to nature then we neglect past generations who set aside this place as holy and tended it as something different to the land around. Instead they seem to be places where we are challenged to live out our faith in our stewardship of them. In a world where we are increasingly failing to recognize our changing relationship with nature, churchyards may represent (as holy places) somewhere where we can do better. They are places where we can witness the cycle of life, remembering our dependence on much more than ourselves.

...earth to earth, ashes to ashes, dust to dust: in sure and certain hope of the resurrection to eternal life through our Lord Jesus Christ, who will transform our frail bodies that they may be conformed to his glorious body, who died, was buried, and rose again for us. To him be glory for ever. Amen.[33]

[33]The Committal' from Common Worship: Pastoral Services (2nd Ed.), Archbishops' Council (London, 2005), p.314.

The Nature of God's Acre: A statistical analysis of the survey results by Miles King

40 parishes were originally selected across the Diocese of Chichester. 17 were selected on the basis they were known to have wildlife value and designated as Sites of Nature Conservation Interest (SNCIs) or where board members had personal knowledge of them. 23 were selected randomly.

175 people responded to the survey, from 25 churchyards in 23 parishes. Of these, 11 churchyards were from the selected parishes and 14 from the randomly sampled parishes.

Age Range (Q2)

Most people who responded to the survey were over 56 and a quarter was over 76.

Age	Number	Proportion (%)
Under 18	1	1
18-35	2	1
36-55	24	14
56-75	104	59
76-90	42	24
90+	2	1

Frequency of Visits to Churchyards (Q3)

People who responded to the survey were most likely to visit once a week. Most visitors (83%) who responded to the survey visited a churchyard at least once a month.

Frequency of visits to churchyard

Frequency of visit	Numbers	Proportion (%)
Every day	11	6
Every year	11	6
More than twice a week	30	18
Once a month	40	24
Once a week	61	36
Once a month	1	
Other, please detail	17	10
Grand Total	**171**	**100**

Seasonality of Visits to Churchyards (Q4)

Most respondents did not tend to visit their churchyards at particular times of year. Those that did, tended to visit in the Summer or Spring.

Season	Numbers	Proportion (%)
Winter	3	1
Spring	21	10
Summer	30	14
Autumn	12	6
All year round	104	49
No particular time of year	42	20
Total (some answered more than one)	**212**	**100**

Reasons for visiting the churchyard (Q5)

The most popular reason people gave for visiting churchyards was when they visited the church for religious reasons. The second most popular was to enjoy a peaceful moment. The third most popular reason given was to enjoy nature.

Reason for visit	All churchyards	Proportion (%)	SNCIs (number)	Proportion (%)
Visit the grave of a loved one	60	13	21	13
Enjoy a peaceful moment	85	19	34	20
Enjoy nature	63	14	28	17
Contemplation/prayer	46	10	19	11
Go for a walk	42	9	15	9
Visit the church (religious)	120	27	44	26
Visit the church (other)	32	7	7	4
Total	**448**	**100**	**168**	**100**

These responses indicate that the most popular reason for visiting a churchyard is when visiting the church for religious reasons, and it is reasonable to assume this means attending a church service. Just over a quarter (27%) of respondents gave this reason. The next most popular reason for visiting was to enjoy "a peaceful moment" (19%), followed closely by "to enjoy nature" (14%). 13% of respondents visited churchyards to "visit the grave of a loved one" and 10% for contemplation/prayer. These figures do not change significantly for churchyards with a known high nature value (SNCIs).

Words that illustrate how visitors feel in churchyards (Q6)
We asked respondents to rank, in order of importance, the words that illustrate how they feel when in their churchyard.

Far and away the most popular words were peace, peaceful, a sense of peace, or peacefulness. This Wordle reflects the relative popularity of each word.

Second choice of word was still dominated by peace, peaceful, etc., but with more people also choosing tranquillity and history, as this Wordle shows.

History figured highly on the third choice of word to illustrate how respondents feel when in their churchyard. Nature figures quite significantly in this 3rd choice.

Some aspect of nature was mentioned in first choice by five respondents, while 15 respondents mentioned nature, including views, in their second choice word. 11 respondents mentioned nature, views, closeness to nature and wildflowers in their third choice word.

When visiting the churchyard, have you noticed the wildlife? (Q7)
95% of respondents said they had noticed the wildlife in their churchyard.

What type of wildlife particularly catches your eye when you visit the churchyard? (please rank from 1 to 7) (Q8)
We asked people to rank the different kinds of wildlife that most caught their eye. 18% of people did rank the different kinds of wildlife. Of these,

Rank	1	2	3	4	5	6	7
Birds	7	7	9	4	2	3	0
Trees	7	7	2	5	7	2	1
Wildflowers	12	6	9	2	2	1	0
Butterflies	4	8	4	10	2	2	1
Other insects	1	4	3	10	10	3	0
Mosses and lichens	2	3	2	7	6	6	6
Toadstools	0	1	1	1	1	6	19

Other wildlife which caught people's eye included slow-worms, hedgehogs and moles.

This shows that of those that ranked the wildlife, wildflowers ranked first as most eye-catching in a churchyard, followed by birds and trees. Toadstools and other insects ranked least eye-catching.

For everyone that numbered different types of wildlife as eye-catching (without ranking them),

Rank	**1**	**2**	**3**	**4**	**5**	**6**	**7**
Birds	54	32	39	16	3	11	2
Trees	82	32	14	10	9	5	3
Wildflowers	61	38	27	11	11	6	3
Butterflies	26	21	24	27	11	10	19
Other insects	11	10	20	20	22	17	26
Mosses and lichens	16	22	25	17	20	22	21
Toadstools	5	7	9	12	9	24	53

Other wildlife which caught people's eye included rabbits and moles.

For respondents who did not rank different wildlife as eye-catching, but gave them scores instead, trees were the most eye-catching, followed by wildflowers and birds.

What type of wildlife do you most enjoy seeing when you visit the churchyard? (please rank from 1 to 7) (Q9)
We asked respondents to rank the type of wildlife they most enjoy seeing when they visit their churchyard.

Rank	**1**	**2**	**3**	**4**	**5**	**6**	**7**
Birds	10	9	10	3	3		
Trees	3	8	8	6	3	4	1
Wildflowers	14	7	7	6	1		
Butterflies	5	7	9	8	0	4	1
Other insects	1	1	2	8	10	6	6
Mosses and lichens	0	1	0	1	11	15	7
Toadstools	0	0	0	3	2	9	17

From the table above, of those who ranked the wildlife, the most popular type of wildlife of which people would enjoy seeing more, is wildflowers, followed by birds. Interestingly very few people indicated they would enjoy seeing more lichens in churchyards, despite churchyards being exceptionally valuable habitats for them.

Rank	1	2	3	4	5	6	7
Birds	69	30	25	8	4	1	1
Trees	67	35	20	13	3	5	2
Wildflowers	77	29	22	9	4	1	1
Butterflies	46	22	27	19	8	1	4
Other insects	17	7	17	22	15	16	13
Mosses and lichens	16	15	10	19	21	28	14
Toadstools	6	7	9	14	11	26	31

Of all those who answered this question, without necessarily ranking the wildlife they enjoy seeing, more people enjoyed seeing wildflowers, with trees and birds close behind. Toadstools and lichens were least likely to be enjoyed. Churchyards can also be very valuable sites for grassland toadstools, such as waxcaps, which are now rapidly disappearing from the countryside.

When you see wildlife in the churchyard, how does it make you feel? (Q10)
We asked people what they felt, by providing them with a list of words, and they agreed or disagreed with that word as appropriate to describe their feelings.

For all churchyards:

	Strongly agree	Mildly agree	Neutral	Mildly disagree	Strongly disagree
Happy	105	26	19	0	3
Relaxed	96	38	12	1	2
Peaceful	106	34	12	0	2
A spiritual feeling	61	42	27	4	6
Thoughtful	57	56	29	1	1
Contemplative	51	50	25	4	3
Sad	6	3	21	18	82
Angry	5	0	9	4	109

For SNCI churchyards:

	Strongly agree	Mildly agree	Neutral	Mildly disagree	Strongly disagree
Happy	27	7	3	0	0
Relaxed	32	10	1	0	0
Peaceful	32	8	3	0	0
A spiritual feeling	24	8	5	0	0
Thoughtful	20	15	6	0	0
Contemplative	18	13	4	2	1
Sad	2	1	4	4	27
Angry	1	0	0	2	33

86% of respondents from SNCI churchyards strongly or mildly agreed that they had a spiritual feeling, compared with 73.5% in all churchyards. 65% of respondents from SNCI churchyards strongly agreed they had a spiritual feeling, compared with 44% from all churchyards.

A Chi-squared test comparing views about respondents having a spiritual feeling when seeing wildlife in churchyards found no difference between SNCI and non-SNCI churchyards.

Is there enough wildlife in your churchyard? (Q11)
Percentage figures in brackets

	All (%)	SNCI (%)	Non-SNCI (%)
Enough	90 (54)	28 (60)	62 (51)
Not Enough	72 (43)	16 (34)	56 (47)
Too much	5 (3)	3 (6)	2 (2)
Total	167	47	120

Slightly more respondents felt there was enough wildlife in their churchyards, but a large minority felt there was not enough. A very small number felt there was too much, and comments mostly related to too many trees, long unkempt grass and moles. For non-SNCI churchyards nearly half of respondents felt there was not enough wildlife.

If you would like to see more wildlife in your churchyard, please indicate which ones you would like to see more of. (Q12)
Percentage figures in brackets

	All (%)	SNCI (%)
Birds	89 (22)	21 (19)
Trees	19	8
Wildflowers	105 (26)	28 (25)
Butterflies	100 (24)	23 (21)
Other Insects	37	11 (10)
Mosses and Lichens	26	10 (9)
Toadstools	20	6
Other	13 (including reptiles mammals, etc.)	3
Total	**409**	**110**

Wildflowers were the wildlife most people wanted to see more of in their churchyards, followed closely by butterflies and birds. Trees were the least popular.

Do you value the presence of wildlife when visiting the churchyard for: contemplation/prayer; visiting the grave of a loved one; enjoying a peaceful moment. (Q14)

We asked respondents whether they valued wildlife while visiting churchyards for other reasons:

Percentage figures in brackets

For all churchyards:

Reason	Strongly agree	Mildly agree	Neutral	Mildly disagree	Strongly disagree
Contemplation/Prayer	64 (42)	48 (31)	30 (20)	5 (3)	6 (4)
Visiting grave of a loved one	59 (44)	31 (23)	35 (26)	2 (2)	6 (5)
Enjoying a peaceful moment	109 (66)	42 (25)	12 (7)	0	3 (2)
All	232 (51)	121 (27)	77 (17)	7 (2)	15 (3)

For SNCI churchyards only:

Reason	Strongly agree	Mildly agree	Neutral	Mildly disagree	Strongly disagree
Contemplation/Prayer	16 (37)	14 (33)	9 (21)	2 (5)	2 (5)
Visiting grave of a loved one	14 (36)	14 (36)	8 (21)	1 (3)	2 (5)
Enjoying a peaceful moment	30 (65)	9 (20)	6 (13)	0	1 (2)

Enjoying a peaceful moment

These results show that the presence of wildlife is most important to churchyard visitors "enjoying a peaceful moment", and those strongly agreeing with that phrase do not differentiate churchyards with known high nature value (SNCI) from the whole sample. The SNCI sample is small compared with the overall sample for this question.

Overall, the proportion of respondents who agreed that they valued the presence of wildlife when visiting their churchyard to enjoy a peaceful moment was 91%, and 85% for SNCI churchyards.

66% of respondents strongly agreed that they valued the presence of wildlife in their churchyard when there to enjoy a peaceful moment.

Contemplation/Prayer

73% (70% for SNCI churchyards) of respondents who used their churchyard for contemplation or prayer agreed that they valued the presence of wildlife when so doing.

42% (37% for SNCI churchyards) strongly agreed that they valued the presence of wildlife when in a churchyard for contemplation/prayer.

Visiting the grave of a loved one

67% (72% SNCI) of respondents agreed that they valued the presence of wildlife when visiting the grave of a loved one, with 44% strongly agreeing. More people felt neutral (20%) about the presence of wildlife when visiting graves than when visiting for other reasons. 44% (36% for SNCIs) of visitors strongly agreed that they valued wildlife when visiting the grave of a loved one.

Statistical Tests

A Chi-squared test was used to determine whether the apparent differences in the value of wildlife when visiting churchyards for different reasons were significant.

Comparison	Chi-squared value	Degrees of freedom	Significance
Peaceful moment compared with other reasons	313.394	4	P<0.001 Significant difference
Peaceful moment compared with contemplation/prayer	29.181	4	P<0.001 Significant difference
Peaceful moment compared with visiting grave of a loved one	20.151	3	P<0.001 Significant difference
Contemplation prayer compared with visiting grave of a loved one			P=0.661 No significant difference

This test indicates strongly that there is a big difference between the way respondents felt about the presence of wildlife when visiting the churchyard to enjoy a peaceful moment, compared with visits for either contemplation/ prayer, visiting the grave of a loved one; or both of these reasons. There was no observed difference in the responses from visits to graves or contemplation/prayer.

Conclusion

Most churchyard visitors who completed the survey were over 56 and this probably accurately reflects the demographic of churchyard users. Most visitors visited at least once a month throughout the year with no particular time of year proving more popular.

The most popular reason given for visiting a churchyard is when visiting the church for religious reasons. A third of visitors stated they visited churchyards to have "a peaceful moment" (19%) and "to enjoy nature" (14%). 13% of respondents visited churchyards to "visit the grave of a loved one" and 10% for contemplation/prayer.

We asked people to choose words to best describe how they felt in their churchyards – the overwhelmingly most popular words were peace, peaceful, peacefulness, tranquil and tranquillity. History, contemplation and various words to describe nature in churchyards were next most important for respondents.

95% of respondents confirmed they noticed the wildlife in their churchyards, with wildflowers being the wildlife which most caught people's eye, followed by birds, butterflies and trees. People also most enjoyed seeing wildflowers and birds in their churchyards, followed by trees and butterflies.

Many people strongly agreed that they felt peaceful, happy and relaxed when they saw wildlife in their churchyard. A large number also agreed to having a spiritual feeling, being thoughtful and contemplative when they saw wildlife in their churchyard.

Slightly over half of all respondents felt there was enough wildlife in their churchyards, but 43% felt there was not enough. A very small number (3%) felt there was too much, relating to concerns about untidiness and moles. People who felt there was not enough wildlife, wanted to see more wildflowers, butterflies and birds in their churchyards. Only a third of people with SNCI churchyards thought there was not enough wildlife, compared to nearly half with non-SNCI churchyards.

We asked people whether they valued the presence of wildlife in their churchyards when visiting for different reasons. People felt much more strongly about the presence of wildlife in their churchyards when enjoying a peaceful moment, than for contemplation/prayer, or visiting the grave of a loved one. 91% of people agreed they valued the presence of wildlife when enjoying a peaceful moment and two thirds strongly agreed. Nearly three quarters of visitors agreed they valued the presence of wildlife in their churchyards when visiting for contemplation/prayer; and two thirds agreed when visiting the grave of a loved one.

Over three quarters of those surveyed agreed that they valued the presence of wildlife in their churchyard, when visiting for these reasons.

Caring for God's Acre

Caring for God's Acre (CfGA) is a national charity with a membership which supports the conservation of churchyards and burial grounds of all faiths and denominations. Whilst recognising and appreciating that the primary function of these sites is for burial, quiet reflection and remembrance, CfGA seeks to support their conservation and enhancement in a sensitive way.

Through the CfGA website, telephone helpline, conferences, training days, case studies and printed information, the charity supports people with the conservation of their own burial sites.

Since the start of the 20th century, old churchyards and burials grounds have become recognised as 'Living Sanctuaries', with many plants and animals finding refuge in sensitively managed sites. The man-made structures, such as monuments and memorials, lychgates and old boundary walls, are of equal importance. It is the presence of both natural and man-made features in a site used for burial and remembrance, which prompts the need for a sensitive and balanced approach to management.

Based on over twenty year's first-hand experience of managing the wildlife habitats and the historic man-made structures within churchyards and burials grounds, CfGA is well placed to help others. These sites can provide a community resource for learning and community activity, particularly around practical conservation tasks, such as grassland and tree care, and traditional skills, such as stone wall repair and scything.

Caring for God's Acre has a simple but effective statement describing its work:

'Protecting wildlife Preserving heritage Involving people'

www.caringforgodsacre.org.uk

info@cfga.org.uk

01588 673041

The People who made The Nature of God's Acre possible

This project would not have happened without the full support of the Bishop of Chichester, The Right Reverend Dr Martin Warner for which we are extremely grateful.

The choice of parishes surveyed was chosen randomly while taking account of a mix of geographical area and of town and rural churchyards. All parishes who took part did so with great enthusiasm and many well beyond what we had expected, without them there would have been no survey and no book and we thank them for their interest and co-operation. During the survey we found many outstanding churchyards of which their parishes are rightfully proud.

The Nature of God's Acre project has been funded by The Spencer-Wills Trust and CPJ Field & Co Ltd, Funeral Directors, of Burgess Hill – we are very grateful for their generous support.

Appendix

This is the questionnaire which was sent to parishes in paper form and made available online

The Nature of God's Acre Questionnaire

The Nature of God's Acre is a project which seeks to investigate the relationship between nature and spirituality in churchyards across Sussex. The project is focussing on the churchyard and the exterior of the church, but not the interior of the church.

Please help us with our survey by filling in this simple questionnaire, which is also available online.

Q1 Please provide the following details.
This information will only be used for the purpose of this survey.

Name of Church
Name of Parish
Your home postcode

Q2 Which age category are you in?

○ Under 18
○ 18-35
○ 36-55
○ 56-75
○ 76-90
○ 90+

Q3 If you attend church, do you ever visit the churchyard? If yes, please indicate how often.
Please select one response only.

○ Every day
○ More than twice a week
○ Once a week
○ Once a month
○ Every year
○ Other, please detail

Further details:

Q4 Do you find that you tend to visit the churchyard more at a particular time of year?
Please tick all that apply.

○ Winter (December – February)
○ Spring (March – May)
○ Summer (June – August)
○ Autumn (September – November)
○ Equally all year
○ No particular time

Q5 Why do you make your visit to the churchyard?
Please tick all that apply.

○ To visit the grave of a loved one
○ To enjoy a peaceful moment
○ To enjoy nature
○ For contemplation / prayer
○ To go for a walk
○ While visiting the church (for religious reasons)
○ While visiting the church (for historical or architectural reasons)

Q6 Please choose three words that best illustrate what you feel when you are in the churchyard, ranked in order of importance
(1=most important)

1 ______________________________
2 ______________________________
3 ______________________________

Churchyards can often be rich in nature, such as birds, animals and wild flowers.

Q7 When you visit your churchyard, have you noticed the wildlife?
○ Yes
○ No

Q8 What type of wildlife particularly catches your eye when you visit the churchyard?
Please rank them from 1 (most catches your eye) to 7 (least catches your eye).

	1	2	3	4	5	6	7
Birds	○	○	○	○	○	○	○
Trees	○	○	○	○	○	○	○
Wild flowers	○	○	○	○	○	○	○
Butterflies	○	○	○	○	○	○	○
Other insects	○	○	○	○	○	○	○
Mosses and lichens	○	○	○	○	○	○	○
Toadstools	○	○	○	○	○	○	○
Other, please specify	○	○	○	○	○	○	○

Further details:

Q9 What type of wildlife do you most enjoy seeing when you visit the churchyard?
Please rank them from 1 (most enjoy) to 7 (least enjoy).

	1	2	3	4	5	6	7
Birds	○	○	○	○	○	○	○
Trees	○	○	○	○	○	○	○
Wild flowers	○	○	○	○	○	○	○
Butterflies	○	○	○	○	○	○	○
Other insects	○	○	○	○	○	○	○
Mosses and lichens	○	○	○	○	○	○	○
Toadstools	○	○	○	○	○	○	○
Other, please specify	○	○	○	○	○	○	○

Further details:

Q10 When you see wildlife in the churchyard, how does it make you feel?

	Strongly disagree	Mildly disagree	Neutral	Mildly agree	Strongly agree
Happy	○	○	○	○	○
Relaxed	○	○	○	○	○
Peaceful	○	○	○	○	○
A spiritual feeling	○	○	○	○	○
Thoughtful	○	○	○	○	○
Contemplative	○	○	○	○	○
Sad	○	○	○	○	○
Angry	○	○	○	○	○

Q11 Is there enough wildlife in your churchyard?
Please select one response only.

○ Enough
○ Not enough
○ Too much

Q12 If you would like to see more wildlife in your churchyard, please indicate which ones you would like to see more of.
Please select all that apply.

○ Birds
○ Trees
○ Wild flowers
○ Butterflies
○ Other insects
○ Mosses and lichens
○ Toadstools
○ Other, please specify

Further details:

Q14 Do you value the presence of wildlife when visiting the churchyard for each of the following.

	Strongly disagree	Mildly disagree	Neutral	Mildly agree	Strongly agree
Contemplation / Prayer	○	○	○	○	○
Visiting the grave of a loved one	○	○	○	○	○
Enjoying a peaceful moment	○	○	○	○	○

Q15 If you agreed with any of the options in Q14, how does this make the experience different?

Q16 We would like to undertake a selection of informal face to face and telephone conversations to further explore these themes in a little more detail. If you would be happy to participate please write your name and a contact telephone number / email address below.
This information will not be used for any other purpose.

Many thanks for your time.